WASTELAND HONEY

also by Robert Clinton

Taking Eden

WASTELAND HONEY

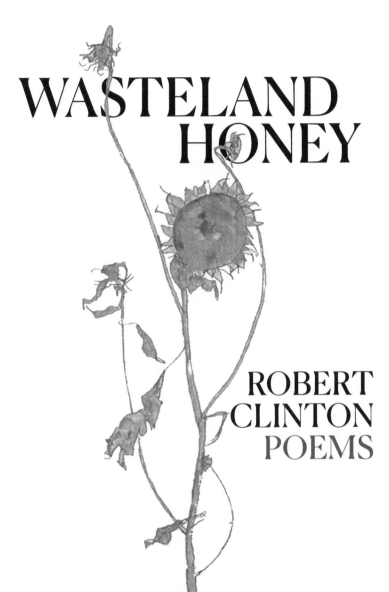

ROBERT
CLINTON
POEMS

CIRCLING RIVERS
RICHMOND, VIRGINIA

CIRCLING RIVERS

PO Box 8291
Richmond, VA 23226 USA

Visit CirclingRivers.com to subscribe to news of our authors and books, including book giveaways. We never share or sell our list.

ISBN: 978-1-939530-19-6 (paper)

Library of Congress Control Number: 2021940062

ISBN: 978-1-939530-20-2 (hardcover)

Library of Congress Control Number: 2021940060

Cover art: Withered Sunflower, by Egon Schiele. Private collection

In "Achieving the Weight": *my cold mad faery father* is from *Finnegans Wake*, by James Joyce

Poems in this collection have appeared in the following periodicals, sometimes in different versions:

Crosswinds Poetry Journal: "Backyards"
Fairy Tale Review: "Harkton's Hundred or, A Wind in the Minagaroons
Hanging Loose: "Then Libya burned" (as "It was then that Libya became a desert")
Jellybucket: "Drug related," "My father's rock pasture"
Lucky Jefferson: "Not what I hear"
Main Street Rag: "With the World Opened to a Page He Likes"
Mudfish: "Pilgrims"
Stand: "Sisyphus in Dedham"

For CF, *in memoriam*

and for Diane, and for Kevin

CONTENTS

IMMEDIATE REQUIREMENTS

COMPANION FACE

SOME FINAL QUESTIONS

If you find you no longer believe enlarge the temple

— W. S. Merwin, from "A Scale in May"

WASTELAND HONEY

SISYPHUS IN DEDHAM

Driving on the six-lane highway
from where I work to where I live
             (want that stone!)
I see a stone has fallen in the grass
on the green verge where the road
chops through a granite ledge.

I want that stone! I go past every day
eighty miles an hour and the stone
has rolled its hundred edges and dark
faces eight feet from the whip of
pavement, and it stands in the dry day
gray glistening split and planed.

Oh how I want that stone –
its mute eight hundred pounds
of mink-black plate and silver gristle
knocked from its socket
by freezing and thawing; in the rain
it glows like a charcoal pearl.

See it going past, fast – want that stone.
I want a man from Maintenance
with canvas-covered chains to lift it
to his flatbed truck and drop it in my yard –
see, there's the porch, here are the two trees
that came with the house.

             O unqualified
and argent stone of dove and frost!
As it has been suddenly faulted away
from its grandfather, and rolled
to the verge of the six-lane highway –
each day I go roaring wanting past –

how I want that stone! Want it!

IMMEDIATE REQUIREMENTS

LAY A RED ROSE

Who it happened to be, stepped
out of nowhere: one day on this
hill she occurred. This woman.
Blackbirds on cattails stood side-
ways, singing their work songs.

I answered *I let everything be*
to her question *What do you do.*
To my question *What do you do*
she said *Chess with the outlaws.*
Breakfast with crows. Each night
my ebony opium pipe. She had
a gold chain and on it a locket –
her own image, her gift. *Keep this.*
Keep us facing. Blue and gray
water, my place, the cattails, peel-
painted rowboat, 80-foot ancient
decayed sugar maple. I told what
I know: *Never in your life will you*
find even one yellow feather from
the red-wing. Her own ivory news:
Lay a red rose on a stone: see how
the stone wall is changed. I gave
us each half a melon, cup of cold
water. I told her *My best swallow,*
my lead swallow, imagines a cube
in the air, 80 feet on a side. Then
in 12 straight lines he flies the cube,
each dusk, each just-failing day.

Whatever carried her now caught
her and lifted, slow over the pond
to touch the pond water, comb
restless reeds quiet, in transparent
air hush in wonder all blackbirds.

CREEK, FIELD

It was a creek that came shining.
To the field the creek gave its water,
green field that faded to yellow away.

A trail to the mast of a tallest oak tree.
Half-handful of rain in a handful of years.
The oak root descending dry miles.

How then can the creek be in water?
– Is a stout cave and filled with old rain,
water over water and six sides of rock

and oak root itself finally rifted the roof
till creek squeezed its jet up the chimney
and the sun takes a drop from the rim.

This old-water creek that comes shining
and to the field the creek gives the water,
green field that opens to flowers always.

SING BACK THE DAY

I take a rose from the vase of roses, a white one; there are red and
yellow roses also. I take a rose from the vase of roses, a yellow one;
there are red and white roses. I take a rose from the vase of roses, a
red one; there are yellow roses and white roses still.

I pull a wagon round a hundred-year maple; there are birches and
sycamores too. I pull the wagon round an eighty-year sycamore; there
are birches and maples too. I pull my wagon round a sapling birch;
there are sycamores and maples as well. The birch will grow tall.

I find a house small as a pocket on a rock; there are ponies, there are
hawks also. A watchful hawk wing-dips at me; here are ponies and
a pocket house too. I find a red pony in spirits; hawks rise in hot air
and the pocket house of bark and moss is occupied.

I find my English tutor in his beehive; my History and my Music
tutors live nearby. I find my Music tutor in his hayloft; my History
and my English tutors pace the ground. I find the balcony where
my History tutor stays; my Music and my English tutors sleep all
afternoon.

I hear my Mother ring the bell; she has a brass horn and a rattling
skin drum also. I hear my Mother tapping on the skin drum; she
sounds the hunter's *going home* on her trumpet and rings her bronze
bell. I hear my Mother pipe the coach horn, shake her bell and rattle
twice her drum.

My father is home the last minutes of day; he rouses the fire and
leans his yew bow on the wall. He leans the tall yew bow and stirs
the fire and daylight is late a few minutes. He makes a high bright
fire; his bow flexes in firelight and in the half-dark he takes my
mother's hand.

He takes a rose from the vase of roses, a white one; there are red and
yellow roses also. I take a rose from the vase of roses, a yellow one;
there are red and white roses. My mother takes a rose from the vase
of roses, a red one; there are yellow and white roses still.

My cot is cool in a breeze; the sun is spent and the birds are dreaming. In my cot in the loft I sing back the day.

BACKYARDS

In the place behind the houses
where the backyards meet,

along the welt cast up by grasses
running down to join the grasses running down
the other way, there isn't
but there ought to be a creek,
between and parallel and under trees.

Dozen lawns roll to the central yellow spine
of weeds their dozen silver greens, where ought
to be a creek, ought to be some child's
manifesto posted on a creekside tree:

*I am the great green ocean
and you are the little yellow boat.*

But along the waste are only knee-high hip-high
strands of brown barbed wire, locust post
to locust post, following the bottoms of the lawns
behind the houses where the backyards meet,
and where ought to be a creek, like this:

I'm walking here. My shoes are soaked and water's
stained my denim black from cuff to knee.
Ahead, a red-wing.

Ahead, somebody's split but fixable canoe.

MY FATHER'S ROCK PASTURE

I sank my house deep in the desert –
the mice rose to eat my bicycle seat.

I steel-staked my house on an ice face –
lost my most meaningful fingertips.

I planted my house on a jungle half-acre –
near lost an eye to the tiniest arrows.

I set the shack back down in my father's
rock pasture – dandelion greens in my

black iron pot and sheep in the house
like cats. Now I walk out with a woman

who promises she'll help me master
many worlds. Thin as a finger, tall

as a silo, she's able and curious and
cheerful and has funds for traveling.

THREE STATES

I hope you enjoy Mexico. I understand it's yellow and black; the
women sometimes brawl; there's one bicycle for fifty children.
A cruel man rules the beaches, but the people bribe the guards
with sweets so they can bathe once a week. In the cities there are
delicious contrasts between the silver people and the golden people
and the living people. Priests in Mexico interfere with numbers, as
in Ireland they jigger the compass. I hope you thrive in Mexico; I
wish I could go with you. I am one-third Mexican.

I hope you like France. The water is rising on the war memorials
but the French still eat better than anyone in the world except
cannibals. The French stay angry at dead people much longer than
their disagreements warrant. They fought heroically in their three
recent wars, with bronze swords. We are indebted to France for
the enigmatic copper figure in New York Harbor. If you do go
to France, be sure to bring back a French child. They are easily
mastered. I hope you go to France at once. It is still lopsided with
cathedrals.

I hope you find a woman to marry in Iceland, although they won't
let you. Right now an Icelandic woman sits in the dining room
of her guest house, writing the menus. Her face is lovely and sad
through the watery glass. Pairs of merlins fly cliff to cliff. Iceland is a
white hat with a flat top and a frayed green brim of fields and sheep.
I hope you like the sunny Icelandic summer nights – they'll give you
a mask for sleeping. My children are Icelanders, the girl more than
the boy. I hope the beautiful Icelandic ponies don't make you cry.

VIGILANCE

i First focus

A child will choose his mother
as soon as he is king of his eyes,
discovering a live attention
that he had none of yesterday.

He follows her rapid fingertips.
He knows her mouth is her voice.
She covers him close with lapped
linens and sings the five flowers.

She inks his frame and copies his
voice to verse. She gives him a door,
teaches him stairs; then, unseen,
marks his way to yonder's green,

but first is the flawless focus of
infant election that orders his eyes.
And his ancient child's heart is
willing to give now, sure as to take.

ii The lice-seekers

after Rimbaud

With manifest sharp silver nails
the sisters come complicit to his bed.
Their fingers wander through his thick
wet hair with lively sly caresses.

They scout for lice: he bears their wary
breaths, diffuse and mild as honey,
the ticking of their tongues, the kisses
of their diligence: they nail the lice.

He sways, suspended lazy listening

to the flutter of their dark eyelashes.
The careful order of their business
excites in him the secret wish to cry.

iii Otto

Date & signature – front or back, nothing else.
I know the writing. The envelope is postmarked
Unreadable. That's Arizona; where he lived.
My address on the envelope is typed. No clue.
One page and smooth as sand. In fountain pen,
as he did always. Date at the top, signature below,
no more. Date is in words, the year is in words.
He's put in the commas. The writing is even
with the straight paper edge. Signature is under-
lined, small ink splash at the end. What am I
not to see? All is odorless. 45¢ flag stamp. Dusty.
Is he – *caught between worlds? Whirling?*
The date: today's date as I'm writing: Sunday,
twenty-two April, two thousand eighteen; signed
at the bottom with its underscore: Otto, his name.
He died in January last year. Not a word since.
If I keep it in a black drawer, maybe the paper
will bubble with print, extra "Ottos" all over.
Maybe news from his alchemists' Eden, maybe
Still got my eye on you. Others will find me –
an out-of-town letter every three or four years,
I predict. Either way, blank page or print, is fine.

for ROC

ACHIEVING THE WEIGHT

my cold mad faery father

I hadn't quite achieved the weight
He hung somewhat upon the ground
and heaving pitching there I struggled
That was a battle and a sacrifice
I was a soldier and a lamb

By noon I hadn't quite achieved the weight
By noon today and noon tomorrow
I had him by the hair and one hand
jammed between his legs he hung somewhat
upon the ground

dragging grooves behind us in the dirt
long legs trying still to walk and carry me

THEN LIBYA BURNED

*Phaeton son of Phoebus undertook to drive his father's solar
chariot, but he fell from the sky, and Libya was parched into
barren sands...*

Today is his birthday. His father will give him
anything he wants. He wants to drive the car.

Father reminds him: The steering wheel is wide
as you are tall. You can't reach the gas, brake,
clutch. You're too little to see over the dash.
He shakes the shift lever. Stiff even in my hand.

With a stick through the spokes the boy shows
how he'll turn the wheel. Wood blocks will raise
the clutch to his toes. *Am I not your son?* Empty
fireworks box on the seat, and I'm tall as the wind-
shield. Proud father, worried, smiling, hymns his
son's inventions to all the gods. But warns him:
your hands off the wheel, you'll fly off the road,
into ditches and grass fires. Wheel in my teeth,
the boy laughs – and half the trip is downhill.

You must ask me for some other thing. Quickly
the boy recites: Give me knowledge and fortune
to know treasure and power beyond your own.
I can't give you this all at once, father answers.
The boy runs inside, to dress himself in leather.
Father elects to ride before him, in front
on his Indian motorcycle. His eyes suddenly shine
with the chance. Three sisters come to the porch
to watch. Car opens its door; the cabin smells
of cedar smoke. Almost the car prepares itself.

And the boy says What if I stay on the road, past
your expectations? What if I trim the stop light
by the brick schoolhouse, swarm into the village?
What if on my way across the plaza I spit into

the fountain? Sisters make a chorus on the porch,
as we've heard: *spit into the fountain, swarm into
the village.* His father shuts the car door: sound
like a hoofbeat on hard earth. A pause for his
Indian motorcycle, taking the lead. Snake rattle
starts the car, shaking its tail,
then cooling to a fluent whisper.

PILGRIMS

We go with the sun carrying our hats our torn-up shirts
Trousers hang ragged and low on our hips our faces burn
and we swing our arms widely to the front to the back

We wear leather boots with the laces untied and we wave
our wide-brimmed hats with the black feathers at the
girls and the sheriffs Our ass-cracks snap like firecrackers

Our belts are long enough They trail us on the road like snakes
Our penis stands between our legs like a sundial Our penis
leads and hardball buttocks follow covered by our low-slung

fire-red pants held by our viper belts and hand-carved boots
the black silk laces trailing in the dust behind and we jump in
a line on the dry rocky road to the chapel of the Fiery Judas

REFUGEE

As we have some padlocked words that need unriddling
and some words understood but ever mispronounced,
so there is a doctor for this
with books and lenses and a wetted cotton handkerchief
to clear your tongue of dottle from the strange mouthfuls.

And if you marry with the native, tied up soon and hard,
she'll spit her words, nor ever let you know her names,
but if you will follow her
with pots and quilts, armloads of firewood, kissing the air,
then she'll make it plain, what she sings but hates to say.

And if you're old, stick-stiff, bat-blind, and nothing from
your bitten hill-town tongue will fold to alien shapes,
there is a woman schooled
in this disorder, who will enlist your glib grandchildren
and buff your lips with flowers, softening the plosive grits

and stacking all the vowels face-front, until it comes to you
to say quietly *I have my own tobacco, thank you,* to say
Here is the little cloth bag with all I could keep.

BY THE RAINBOW HERBICIDE TANKS

Father's an old wooden bucket filled with weeds.
Mother's a red round potato with sprouted eyes.
One child is motored alive with titanium gears.
One child dusts his brain every night before sleep.
The messenger brings gifts of masks and gloves.
The baby on the floor is eating red and gold bugs.
And grandfather: clothes soured by ill-advised milk,
he's rusty-spoked, like a bicycle buried ten years.
Grandmother flies out from the cupboard, chirps
like a sparrow, brown dotted wings brush the ceiling.
Whole placid family on the floor playing cards.
Cards have a front and a back: that's all they know.
Round red potato deals six dozen cards everywhere.
Nobody knows how to win – long peaceful game.
Hair comes in orange on the children's lead heads.
In the yard the puddles change shapes like amoebas.
Three-headed headless blackbirds and red rabbits
all drunk from wood barrels of stupefacient syrups.
The messenger delivers broad-spectrum antibiotics.
One child buries his head in his chlorine pillow.
One child every night admits to a new blue bruise.
The man's an old wooden bucket of weeds, of weeds,
and his wife's a rusty potato sprouting eyes all over.
They clitter and clatter upstairs, get into their bed
and sleep: all noisy night their difficult breaths.
The children bide, knowing nothing of toxic semen.
What bubbles their brains weeps from the tank lids,
seeps out the Union-made seams: unlucky house-
holders – deliquescent kittens on the front steps.
She sleeps under a silver-spattered shawl. He's
rigged like a doctor: three feathers, shell necklace.

AT DOCTOR'S

He takes off the bandages that last week
he laid on the old lesion I bravely bear.

He removes the slightly damp cloths, damp
from my thoughts, which embarrasses me.

Is a new inflammation? may beg for a new
dye needled in or a new design needled on,

to brain via eyes – my queries how they're
used, how they work, not answered precisely

or at all. Me hooded again, we settle to talk.
He waits while I tie knots in my tongue,

saying what I've lived, this week what I've done –
in briefest half-truthful details – him planning

the ten solo minutes he's saved shrewdly
to dust me away now my survival's assured,

spite the toy box my madonna kept locked,
spite my father's preposterous algebraic

mustaches – Doctor indites the prescriptions
that my druggist will inspect with distaste –

wetted bandage pressed firmly, not visible in
sun or moon light. And Doctor asks, Next time

we meet, can I have a few friends in? – then
Doctor's door & twenty-six steps to the street.

SYSTEM SWEEP

Let the night stars be dusted and polished; let day stars
be wiped and waxed, though they're unseen. Manage
the system's beast of a star with a vigorous abrasive
buffing. Sheer off the littlest flame-trees, and the largest,
highest arches of light and fire, rabid parabolas, bed
them in thick cool plasma. A filthy lost place they left it.

Keep the Moon close. She'll ignore our remarks about
her pocked and hatcheted face – still famously,
delicately white. We'll set her to novel phases – *new* and
old and *borrowed* and *blue*. Timely as the Sun, carelessly
outshining the stars: neighborhood's favorite, she calls
up the water, does the Moon, when there's water to call.

And Earth, like a mother's angry about-to-speak face:
drag this ruined one up close. A filthy lost place they
left it, scorned and burned and sick all over itself.
We'll bring a celestial water-pumpkin, knock it to pieces
a hundred miles up; after a few years some cold rain
will fall, but later see the harsh face weeping with floods.
We'll compose new models of trees that can fight.
When rivers and floods have burnished the landscape,
then come the new types, now in beta, masterwork
assemblies from perfected wombs, eager for knowledge
including, we'd guess, templates for further extinctions.

HARKTON'S HUNDRED *or* A WIND IN THE MINAGAROONS

I walked by Harkton's Hundred
where the froyn and the quirts are flowering,
and I've never seen greener dewstein
than what flows over Harkton's pastures.

The lazy and poignant froyn deploys in its
tissues and twigs a scented air, distantly,
faint copy of the flowers, but it says *You come*
here and leads you to the southeast corner
where it was pridefully set by Dissenters.
Busily it spin-sings its gray and white flowers:
froyn's fragrance comes in a private coach.
I felt scent-induced vertigo, standing so close.

Quirts, or hackroot, a tough blooming hedge,
has got Harkton's Hundred onto its grid,
bounding his fields in sharp straight lines.
Quirts comes to spring in a scarlet coat
of tiny odorless florets; the coat falls in May
and here are the little quirts leaves, simple
hearts of bright green, mint-smelling, liking
well to be pruned in the fall: politely a fence.

And the dewstein is deep and constant on
Harkton's lawns and pastures. It roars and
rolls everywhere, burying tree stumps, over
your doorsill and into the front hall, half
masking the apple tree trunks. A bluegrass
in color, but dewstein is bluer and grassier.
It holds to the ground so close and floods our
fields like thick green paint or billows of sea.

I walked by Harkton's Hundred
where the froyn and the quirts are flowering,
and I've never seen dewstein so lush
as what flows over Harkton's pastures.

I waited to see if Harkton was home – would he
open the door with *Good Morning,* or was he
down in the Hundred somewhere, recking with
last fall's pommeley briars that lock to your
fence rails, at least till the phoebe wasps come
and drain the new shoots – or was one of his
herd of premiere bowhas not being correctly
an animal – pails of songs instead of true syrup?

It's a rich-dirt farm but nobody home, Harkton
or Lady Dame Harkton or the sons, still twins after
all these years. A wind in the minagaroons, that
hang their blue blooms from the rafters, and pink
mandaleets sang through the trees. I hatted myself
and took the north road. I'd spend a dime at Mrs.
Dotspot's for three of the jelliest ling-dings in town.
I'm doing that, walking uphill with my dime.

WAMPEQUOT FRAGMENT

A few of us bateau'd down Wampequot
where it falls apart through the marsh
in a handful of channels to the bay, not
one with its former resident blue heron.

Dry spartina bowed in the on-shore wind.
Coils of Wampequot sank in sand, shed
skins of trash. Food chains were tangled,
grease grass fermenting, sugar and sand,
80 proof tide pools. Wax bubbles popped
off the water – lethal – in Babylon colors.

We put in error our boots into pools of
bright orange and green water, so warm,
rots cloth in seconds, kills periwinkles,
blue mussels, sea stars, crabs and fair
venomous anemones. Boots sticky with
blinded dead foundlings from miscarried
tides, fingers opened by razor-reeds, day
grayed by a smoky sun, we climbed onto
dry sand and watched curiously the grand
ancient ocean being trimmed and focused.

Then our brother, home from diminished
eternal Himalayan snows, bewildered us,
saying, At the equinox, unveil your eyes:
some essential spring engines have failed
or belong now to a different time. My own
team brought daisies down from South Col.

The bay was rigid with tankers, the tankers
were alive with guards, the guards were
artificially watchful as the tankers were all
empty and sat high in the black bay water.
That was the day a few of us bateau'd down
Wampequot, one native word for unreason.

WASTELAND HONEY

The sun still recalls the colors.
Stars pin up black canopies,
seem to leap into their places
half-seconds before you look.
Sunset, and all the barns burn.

April's green axis pierces the waste
with lone pickets of sorrowful bloom.

At blown dams and lost lakes
sharp sand is to swim in. Wild
rocks and beasts in rich gravel –
wagons spun round in a vortex.
Winds shake the pied shanties.

Human shoes wind and waver along
the dry rumpled and red dirt paths.

Kids are up early, wringing dew
from the moths. They still clap
when the stars snap to their
frames. Before noon and after,
the babies are keeping the bees

in the waste, for the wasteland honey.
Cornflowers in dry furrows, rare blues.

Mice drown in the dust. Kids go
to school in hollow trees with no
water for baths or kisses. Every
day some small human figures
are removed from the drawing.

Bedtime: from an ancient glass jar, one
honey-dipped finger on each child's lips.

NOT WHAT I HEAR

What bell is ringing, in pastures and plazas?
Is it High Street shops ringing retail bells –
bells calling for commerce? Aching for drugs,
for fast-cooked not-food and the pizza slice
everybody's got in his pocket?
But the bell that I hear isn't for retail or trade.

Or police, loudest men on the planet? – yelling
See the sign, stupid? can't you read braille? Or
car wheels banging steel road plates, or Jacks
in back-hoes, dim figures in crane cages lost
among fifty-one gears, tooting
their reverse alerts? but that's not what I hear.

I hear the iron ring in all sectors, all precincts.
Not house alarms chasing thieves; not church
bells calling the bad hats to kneel on hot tiles
& send caustic prayers to the author of all evil,
or the jingle of ice cream trucks
placidly trolling the streets – you hear it; that's

not what I hear. I hear the black day-and-night
tolling, almost too loud and too deep to bear.
It will beat without cease in pastures and plazas
till unlikely reason is born out of fury, and all
of the living are licensed to laugh,
& every impassive national Nero has vanished.

TOWN PICNIC

Sadie killed Mother.
Father killed Mother twice, right here in the church.
Mother killed Billy.
Hank killed Father in his coffin between two stones.
Father killed Sadie.
Mr. Boch killed Mother with a pellet to her withers.
Sadie killed Father.
Aunt Bessie killed Sadie standing on her with her car.
Sadie killed Billy.
Hank killed Father with a long red monkey wrench.
Sadie killed Aunt Marples.
Mr. Boch killed the Priest Bobby with a toxic wafer.
Billy killed Father.
Mr. Boch from a tree killed Hank with shot of nuts.
Aunt Marples killed Aunt Bessie.
Billy killed Hank in the street with peroxide and ants.
Sadie killed Mr. Boch.
Father killed Sadie, he took and he buried her to death.
Hank killed Aunt Marples.
Billy drowned Priest Bobby, left him floating like a log.
Mr. Boch killed Sadie.
Father killed Mr. Boch twice, once up from each end.
Mother killed Father.
Hank killed Sadie with a wind-up poison rattlesnake.
Billy killed Aunt Bessie killed Billy.
Mother killed Mr. Boch all over town with her slingstones.
Mr. Boch killed Father.
Father killed Mother in the pink bedroom with a pillow.
Sadie killed the Dogs.
Mother killed Sadie until her head was the size of a baseball.
Hank and Billy killed everyone.

Then the Mayor stood up in his hood and ended the games.
Hank stopped killing Billy.
Sadie undid all her murders and put on a bright yellow dress.
The Priest Bobby was stood up

and dripping wet he prayed and thanked a puissant Almighty.
On the church porch
Mother and Father, their arms around each other's waists,
thought *Wait till next year.*

AT THE ROADHOUSE, WITH THE IMMORTALS

Kronos, who is wicked with his father's nut-blood.
Zeus his son who is bull and cuckoo and swan.
Aphrodite, sea-splash from Uranus' genitals cast.
Adolescent *Ares*, detested by soldiers.

Four travelers discovering a congenial roadhouse
– on tap, that thick black ambrosia, kegged in oak.

The son sighs *Mortal women!* – snapped fingers,
snake lightnings. Kronos-clock-face acidly drools
abuse. Morose armored teen with a million-dollar
car: him killing all the days with street nomads.

Bump into their table, they'll freeze your socketed
bollocks. They spring up at slights, they never sleep,
they have no intimates and take no shit. Asks fretful
elder, *What am I eating?* Who cheats with cows rudely,

disdainfully, dutifully tells him, *More meat pies, old
cannibal, one after the other, and finally a stone.*
Here's that daring new Canaanite band! Old Time
dances solo, complexly shuffling. His law-giving

youngest and author of much corrupt flesh stands
up with a tavern girl: they dance and the room gets
smaller and smaller. And contrary to your doctored
photos, the boy is fourteen and still scared of spiders.

The beautifully salted girl asks of young steel-teeth,
won't he play cards. Assyrian tambourines ring the
popular song – a ballad of a comic live burial. *Where
hies my speckled thrush* sings the sea-fetched girl,

calming a fourteen-year fury. Cards of ivory and wood
played in twos and threes. *Where hies my thrush and*

the night so cold? – and the Sun rises. Eight sandals
climb the fire stairs, leather neat and hung with bells.

Each evergreen figure is brilliantly scented with incest.
They walk nimbly to the sky, and more, since they can.

WITH THE WORLD OPENED TO A PAGE HE LIKES

On the ridgepole, a mockingbird
Among the nettles, red admirals

A man is running out of his uniform,
the road dusty, his face shoulders and hips
white with dust

A woman is jumping up and down on the porch
hands to her cheeks
shouting to someone behind her

FLINT GIRL

What if I carry you up Saddletop Ridge?
They say at the peak there's the foundered wreck of a steamboat.
What if I take you to hear women sing?
They say a man calls out from the seats with a breaking heart.

What if I take you to my carpenter's shop?
They say the machines' malevolence will spit out your fingers.
What if I take you to the Mile-High Pylon?
They say if the Pylon reaches a mile it can have no substance.

What if I take you to the rowdy Bal-Musette?
They say people are liable to hysteria, jumping around suchwise.
What if I take you away from your cowboy?
They say there's never a darker sound than a cowboy's sad song.

What if we walk in the head-high corn?
They say the view is much greener in the short-cropped meadow.
What if a blanket in black woods, flint girl?
They say there's a chapel with a priest who'll marry us, for cash.

QUICK TO THE BONE

I've walked along, seeing no one,
and I've walked along, with no sign,

and it's good. I sleep in the leaves,
long gone stars scratched above me.
It's good. All fires out but this one.
Loved broken things fell off as I ran,
whole parts of human discarded, not
wanted, in dry pools, yellow waters.

I've walked far away, seeing no one,
and I've walked far away, with no sign.

It's good. No further use for things:
for red rocks erect at the noon-hour
sun-shaft, for drums, for whistles.
I've claimed a place, made it flat,
keep it swept, half asleep, half awake,
head on my sack of black leaves –
see no one: it's good: hear no one.
Bodies in piles like little blue stones
even when some could still move and
still speak. Now this is the high plain,
this combed swept solitary place.

I've walked over waste, seeing no one.
I've walked in what's left, with no sign.

I'm last of these dancers: I've chanted
and eaten the fire – now I'll wittingly
starve and then sensibly burn. Loved
nothings without names fall to their
atoms, even now, after all, silent and
quick to the bone and then done. It's
good. Nothing else. None come or go.

UNSEEABLE BOXES

He walks to a locked metal building where are
thousands of sealed small rooms: death at dawn.
In each room is an agent who knows the modules,
knows the bits to uncable, collects floaters, clear
drifting tissues – the unfinished fractions circling
these incompletely annihilated units; the agents
are muting and firing the scraps. And faint sprays
of sense, robust but exhausted – gallant atoms
to break down in sunlight, in sun rooms. It's these
detailed more final extinctions this death verifies,
realizes in full. Death finds determined Mayday
transmitters hidden in tiniest vacuums, still
preaching anathemas. For them, eternal life with-
out existence is ordered. *I'm done with this one,
Pop,* says an agent – death delves: for some missed
mosaics of sound, undone soliloquies, signifying
fingerprints. Air fidgets; death is calm, no matter
the scale heroic or the scale sub-atomically small.
Thousands of times each day they pack nothing
into unseeable boxes; these are thrown into deep
space, past death's own dacha and hammered sun.
Death smartly sweeps. Agents sign by the clock.
Death carries nothing. No day does he stop doing
death: that's all he does. He'll do it to you. Imagine
how many of him there must be.

NOW I WILL HAVE MY PEARL

I was put back to a moment just before birth, and this
is what I heard my mother say, as if through clouds:

What will it be, that we've made me carry? And my father answered,
It's head and body, one boy. They sat gravid and solemn each side of
a fire, plates and glasses, food and water. Not afraid.

Then my mother said from outside and above where I was hotly
pocketed: If I could, he'd be pure eastern Kentucky. But I come off
a list two thousand centuries old, a film, a long band of lace. I came
with mine frayed and filthy, yours no more cared for, but it blew me
up to this impossible bulk. Now the boy waits. You hear him wait.

I barely could feel my father speak from inside my mother's waxy
distended middle, me cabled, sensible, sprouted and heaving. Surely
he put calm hands to her face, and his feet were flat on the floor,
though the house was rocking. He said, Our uninterrupted lines,
unstopping, impalpable, slipped through the grass and the ice and
the sea, collecting tattoos and scars, timeless, indelible, until there
was your egg, transparent only to me. This head and body of a boy
we carry will take his manners from each breed and blood.

I think my mother leaned back in her chair; this eased the weight
from my unsewn head-bones, from my slow waving limbs. Her
voice was close and hushed. Does God manage the thing as it starts,
she asked; does He declare appearances? Is part of it His to keep?
Will prayer minutely spark and then kindle the soul – and will we
know the child well as a man?

My father answered my mother, his voice coming faintly as if from
across five fields: I don't know that. I don't make prayers. And god
is later; he's lazy; he has for his leaping particular pleasure yearly
attacks upon new-sprung Sodoms. God appearing in the grain
fathers awkward discontinuities. Soon whom you carry will begin
preparing himself to be unhoused, red and withered and complete:
maybe blue bronze eyes, maybe his hair copper-red, a strong marker
from your houses and clans. My mother laughed; I was shaken.

Now sounding from deep in a well my mother said, I'm going to lie down – this boy to me so strange will no doubt come in off the street, knock at the door; you'll listen for the knock. Or maybe tonight God will uprise and sign his soul, and he'll pour out of me, liquid and corded and crying, his ancient fathers pointing out all his million-year parts – the scar of his disconnection, tattoos of his opened eyes, the soft chant of his breathing.

But my father: The faulty motor rebuilt once more, and sacks with the weight of human debt to carry, and chimeric speculations, and the lived life suffered until the ultimate fire. I could hear my father whispering so, as to the bedroom my mother heavily walked, and climbed on the bed to wait, saying *Now I will have my pearl:* this I distinctly heard, as I was no more among their organs.

Thus was I put back to a moment just before birth, and then delivered again to my age, by hands I can't recall or address.

IMMEDIATE REQUIREMENTS

To have the car door opened
To skate across the busy street

To enter the building
in a state of romantic unclockiness

To be kissed by the oldest waiter
in the bar and, leaving little footprints
of flame

to head for the table in a distant corner
where a man sits
wealthy with drugs sex and art

LOVE SONG

He hits and I collapse
and you collapse
His steps delight me
I have all his records

I'm in charm

His engineer's gown
torn up the back –
it's simple that he sits
and leaves blood:

pity him

His voice after his cough
scratched and sweet as violin
I get sleepy
from so many ways he's weak

In myself I leave the light on
that he may carry me ahead
into his danger: I love a man
with two hands

My phantom breasts love
and my device of a cup
I leave on his step

Terror me to lose him

EVENING PRAYER

after Rimbaud

I lie in the chair like a fat man waiting for a shave,
all fat neck, fat belly and a beer pot with a thick
glass bottom in my hand and hookah in my teeth,
expanding through the room, my sails and smoke.

All evening daydreams drip their caustic through
my heart, so its four birds murmur in their cages –
they see each other's come and go of blood, brown
blood and black, me mournful and bad-tempered.

Then the swallowed flame jumps south and burns
my bladder. Fragrant water there begins to boil
and I stand up, nearly, grabbing for the doorframe,
and piss the whole horizon, very high and very far.
The spatter on the grass and gravel wakes my dog,
and midnight heliotropes exhale a blue applause.

TOBACCO

– We went to the smoke shop on Haight Street. We had half a dollar for Luckies. A flatbed truck blocked the street by the park. Kids set the amps and ran cables. Then proud longhairs jumped up with guitars and ice cream and tambourines and keyboards. Grateful Dead. They played all afternoon. What a thing to have seen.

– Listless and damp, he peered idly through periscopes and scraped mud from his tongue and cursed, morning and night. At last came the forgotten allotments of cigarettes. Soon he was writing poems in his journal, organizing a Jubilee, singing the Marseillaise. He was killed twice. The War ended abruptly for three more years.

– A savage amity erupted with the first draw on the pipe. The Major took too much, but managed it. He noticed a boy in the background drawing on deerskin. Someday those pictures will be all the Nation I have, the Chief said in a savage resigned voice, and that scribbler's grandson will dance knowing nothing. They all took smoke.

– After four generations the coffin was opened. An acorn-sized body: G. Washington. As well in the coffin, a cache of the finest old bright-leaf aromatic and rum-soaked cigars, the most warming, dizzying, lip-sticking stogies in the world. – Well, how we blessed his lucky childhood in his father's cherry orchard!

– As Embellisher to the King, I have opportunities to observe his temper. Evenings he smokes his long French cigarettes, made with the amber leaves from St. Pathetica. These promote his clear reason and inquisitive spirit. I'm writing his memoirs: my book will be praised for its method. The King's eyes sparkle when they give him his dog.

– The finest Italian villas are shaped in spirals; in the tip of one spiral arm is a room where scholars relieve the anxieties of argument with tobacco smoke. These years Fra Spezio wrote the *Appezio*, a verse Tract Against Farmers. It took him 7 hours to smoke his last cigarette. He was shot by a mother and her sister's four sons, using the Carcano M91/38.

– In centuries nine through eleven, time without past, without future, people lived only 26 years and God said, *You live short and ugly because I'm learning, too.* Writing was rare and construed suspiciously by monks with powers to tip the earth over. But St. Tabac of the Ways had his agents, and he would return with his anodyne.

– Four centuries below Zero, four centuries above, tobacco and verse and wine built several dozen civilizations: for example the often deranged Greeks, the splendid Persians, the mawkish hissy Romans. Jesus sewed tobacco leaves inside his robes. The children learned to make adobe. The Mayan land bridge to Ireland was begun.

– Up the gray rock one thousand feet: steady your eyes on the crack that's a shelf: a man sits on the edge, feet dangling. See how he marks the tablet on his knees with precise painted words which mean what he sees, and look, there's a clay pipe in his mouth, from which he inhales a few daily breaths of smoke. Soon, this will be China.

– In plated and re-plated Egypt, where all surfaces, even the infinite sands, were recklessly inscribed, urchins on the Boulevards offered guilty cigars to urchins from the Avenues, who rinsed their mouths with myrrh-water before going home to their mud houses to paint poems on the palm-leaf curtains.

– In the seventy cities of Sumer, there were tobacco festivals, during which sins and debts were forgiven. Only priests and noble families could use tobacco, although smugglers sold folded four-foot leaves after dark. Recently translated texts yield regular instances of the use of tobacco during fatal Sumerian bicycle races.

– Plates of ice descended the valleys. Families moved south. Clans already feeding on southern lands disappeared. The People sat at the fire, dressed in elephant robes and bark derbies. A man lit up a smoke and passed it around. Their speech, unlike the earth, was heavy with flowers. They had a word *charcoal*, words *daisy* and *someday.*

DRUG-RELATED

As the medicines snap to their places,
or drive through my blood, victorious,
I know. I hear the handcuffed shuffling
lipids. Mountain Rescue rappels down
long muscles, re-weaving what's torn.
Boats trawl my synaptic clefts, drag
transmitter molecules back to their
weathered gray channels, forwarding
ambiguous information and if-then
data incessantly – some dozen pellets
and spoonfuls a day successfully keep
my whole person vexed and charged.
Not do this – organs in despair cease
signaling the editorial brain. Formerly
quiet cooperative small units succumb
to their most hideous ambitions. Deny
the filled spoon, dodge potent pharma-
seeds – I'll burst like a random thistle.
So I'm eating what keeps me upright,
with plenty of honey. When it's my time
to burn, I won't wait in line to see views
of Paradise, or watch saved ones follow
their angel pilots, avid for drugs for the
eternal sick of regret.
                        Someone will taxi
my frame downtown – I'll shake red-
eyed firemen's hands; fair firemaids I'll
kiss. Now my earth reclines; then by a
button will be fire. Farewell, I'll imagine,
to constant unknowingness; valedictions
I'll dream, as I'm able, to the highest and
wrong true things: meaning blood and
thought and honey. Someone will stand
away, and all my ports will be stormed.

COMPANION FACE

FINAL CABIN

I'm here for the bounties of rain,
for the fifty-five gallon drums of sun
overturned in the fields. I'm here
under midsummering stars, raising
a final cabin. When it's done
my little house in town will disappear.

Posts need to be forced, cut not quite
true, and carrying bundles of shingles
up to the roof bewitches my breath
some days. Mornings a pony, then noon,
surprised, solo and almost a greybeard:
two canes, them both solid amber.

I've stolen stones dropped by ancient
ice sheets. Under hemlocks I've burgled
shacks to the ground – you'll see grieved
cabins I've thieved. Wood pups – pup
foxes, pup rabbits – Hark, I call them,
come live here with me.

Say that you're ticketed, say soon you'll
be sailed up the Sound by enormous
Marines and put down on the granite
land-handle at my beach with a book,
a soap, a compass and string-bags
of clementines. Come soon, soon.

Late afternoons if there's nothing
irritably undone, I dream of your cheerful
command of carpentry. The Ten Stout
Lamas' *Ten Wanderings from Meaning* –
bring that. I'll dust you with joy. I'll
have found joy somewhere. Come soon.

DEEP INTO SIMPLE

Tastes I didn't know until your time here –
now I know what might grow in the waste:

blue poppy seeds, white willow bark, blends
Arab and Celebes, palk from the palk marsh,
fairy green absinthe and filaments of amber –
they fall on the tongue, they fall in the palm,
almost more tall tales than tastes.
Until your time here, we'd not cared to know.

Until you taught how to see deep into simple,
powerful manshaped Gods lived everywhere.

We gave you a house in a field, with an oak.
Mornings you taught us the meadow's Greek.
I watched you rub leaves, hissing handfuls
you spilled in the soup. You brought the tools:
See your cutting and digging is done to a beat.
We hadn't yet cared for such pioneer things.

Now you're leaving: is it to scatter your soft live
lectures abroad? This plain place still too hard?

Or is it my folly to admire your consequence?
I'll stand out of your path if you'll speak to me.
Could my affection keep you – could it be zest
of roses and bourbon vanilla, your house in a
field, new stories, green lessons, new spirits?
I'll wait at the stone that you'll have to go by.

ROSE-CLEAN

Here's a bucket full of water from our old rain barrel,
and there's sliced black bread in the safe. Tonight
you can have your bed solo, or stay here and love me.

With me you'll be thirsty in a while and need to drink.
There's a cupful of rain barrel water on the chair near
the bed. You'll be hungry, not wanting to eat all of me,
and there's a loaf of black bread and jam in the safe.

If you sleep solo, with a thimble of water, I'll know stair-
flights away how sadly you rest, how sorry you'll wake.
Narrow in your bed, if you're mud-deep in loss I'll know:
you'll take just the crust and the seeds. I won't stir

from my housekeeping: making the bed like a fortress.
Later in candlelight I'll watch you asleep and I think
you'll watch me. After sunrise we'll swim, we'll walk all
the fences. You'll cinderella me; I'll get the ladder that

tops the thorn trees. I'm rose-clean, vigorous, fragrant.
In my mouth still are sweet drops from the rain barrel.
The moon will whiten these dusty sheets: indeed it will.

PICTURE BOOK

It's no trespass, in sorrow, making a song
for the woman whose youth is a laid away
ornament, her life bricked up to the eyes –
a few years left to enjoy faith's anxieties;
nor untoward mutely to imagine her heart's
preserve, read through her studies of loss,
look for her alloy pride, know her affections
were fully returned, many times and again.
A beauty so bright and plain; colt's quiver
when she closed with you. Follow the trail
of her words one inch away from her kiss.
Her fair face was the lamp she held steady –
then it lit up like a child's book of pictures.

Now she has time, now her children can
fly, she searches her long-lined meditations
for verse, drops in chasms wrong couplets,
taps a drum for what's true. So what if new
elegant voids rise up, white, unnumbered.
I heard madness is perfect memory. I'm not
mad, minding our put-away days – I don't
recall certainly warm lips or cool, blue eyes
or brown. I know the shadows are doubled –
just one is the sun's. We treat with what is,
and we puzzle at what is no more.

EMBELLISHING AND CAROLING

Salute and felicitate the masters who are gone,
who had the rage and grace to solve the world
with abundant false and half-true histories,
with paints to weave a girl's red braided hair,
or melancholy echoes by the cello of contagions
in the fevered heart.
        Their images in clouds will
shake shambling into life again: I'll hear them,
embellishing and caroling. Mephisto footprints
punch the rocks where they once stood vexed:
look again to where they might walk presently,
bending to a rigor their necessary servants.

SNOW SIEGE

Then something banged on my house
and from the sound, it must surely have
shattered shingles, and branches crashed
against the windows hard enough to break
the glass, and heavy guns came fumbling
up the driveway, blasting at my porch
and at my front door, certainly destroying.
I could hear huge iron-mine earth movers
lift and turn it must have been my whole
yard front and back and down to bedrock.
I kept vigilant, at a height above sleep.
Soon, whatever forced my house
disengaged. Branches hooked tight
to their trees again; wheeled cannon,
spiked, rolled downhill toward town,
and mammoth scoops and drills withdrew
from my convulsed and aching yard -- all
outside was still, or just murmuring night
birds unheard before, wiry winds, clear skies
baptized with stars. Next daylight
I surveyed the damage: shingles whole un-
scratched all over the house, no broken
glass, front door stout and latched, yards
calm with unturned snow. I don't mind this
vaudeville storm. Final weather is mute.

SO WHAT

I'm too wild with it now to write all I'm thinking,
but I need to say that I saw her tonight, in her skin,
on the street. It was her; she was here in life again,

black boots and bare knees, carrying books and
records, silvery wrist coils and coming home late.
I could see her inward eye and her rustic red

mouth. She walked fast away to her someplace.
She was entire – yellow hair and light as a moth,
her new and her old parts finished and clothed.

I doubt she saw me at all, standing there staring
in the middle of the sidewalk, hands hanging with
nothing. From a red saloon, through its opening-

closing doors, came patches of her elected song
– *So what* – every day she listened to him say *Don't
be dishonest* – she said they had rain in common.

High Street shops are brilliant downtown noon-at-
night with thousand shadows. I walked from there.
I see life is losing. I see every life is a loss to come.

A FIRE ON THEIR TONGUES

I went to the man who sells flour, the miller, I said Please –
I said to the man who sells butter and eggs, the farmer, I said –

and then a big bowl up here where I can be sitting and stirring.
Took hold of a spoon; I'm making a great white cake for them.

Not that I know how cake is made, but to make a cake, this cake,
you need a whisk and I'll use a lily out of a pail, a pale white lily.

I have my cake things: coal-hard sugar-flour, my own spices &
pulled roots that will leave a rosy blue stain on each silver fork.

Now my cake flowers inside the fat oven, seven round layers,
seven mortared steps, the broad knife for the icing and nothing

tastes *mental*. On top, the candied Bride, the stiff candy Groom,
and when I say *Stand* they stand up, their wide open eyes on me.

O! the family's temper smolders as I unbidden walk a brick walk
to the table: *This gift of a large cake I got with farmer with miller.*

O! and how nasty and hungry! Surprised and bitterest welcomes!
Some people tell lies and a fire on their tongues, some people not.

I feed no one and I urge no one to eat but by sunset,
him and her and all of them, every beast on the estate:

they partake – of my cake

and fall down asleep. Crows overhead upside-down float neatly
into piles of shavings: crows and a bear! all sleeping, asleep!

I arrange their feet with another lily from the pail. I load their
sleeps with one-hundred-year dreams of false awakenings.

I step from the highest window and fly conspicuously home.

I JUST STOPPED FOR GAS

she has a red ribbon
she has a nice hair
she has a bold rise
she has a pretty face
she has a good Ma
she has a nice legs
she has a *you know*
she has a red Camaro
she has a Oreo cookie
she has a short shorts
she has a Payday one hand
she has a OJ other hand
she has a saddle tan
she has a Ma in the garden
she has a *picture of you*
she has a flat belly
she has a high shoulders
she has a smile your way
she has a Ma explains Time
she has a way of *seeing you*
she has a nice hands
she has a bliss smile
she has a key to the carousel
she has a note from the moon
she has a dog loves her Ma
she has a *picture of you*
she has a nice knees
she has a thing that counts
she has a handful of bees
she has a long stride
she has a rich mixture
she has a lively burn
she has a racer's pivot
she has a two-mile start
she has a *you're looking at her*
she has a pretty face

she has a thing that counts
she has a *you're looking at her*
she has a Oreo cookie
she has a picture of you

THE BLUE EQUESTRIAN

So much do we care for each other,
we change names a dozen times in a day,
so we can meet again, introduce, and kiss.
We memorize all the other one knows
of the world, even sorry things far past
repairing. We care for each other so hard,
we mock the lions' rough pleasures and
shame the binary stars. A white house
with a greenhouse, a ball field, an oak –
and if there are wrong parts, you'll care
for the wrong parts, while the right parts
are caring for you. Our favorite movie is
The Blue Equestrian In Scarlet Weather.

FROM A MEADOW

I kneel in the meadow with my stick and my sleep.
I'm a clean yellow spot and I'm happy and mortal
in impassive air with its motionless beads, leaves
gloved and still, birds happy to pause and consider.

Stones rolled from stone walls into idle green grass,
onto heavy soft earth. The broken cow barn, walls
slipped off their piers, stalls varnished with animal
oils. Within laboring voices and powers I've been:

no more. Here are snakes in the sun without steam;
here are locusts expelled from the chorus, the chorus
disbanded. The daisy, the fly and the distant coal
train alike settle. A cottontail not hidden from me,

though it's hiding. Water drops stop, blue poppies
bow low to my hand as I lodge in the long narrow
meadow, a patch of what wraps up the earth's rock
wheels. Ruthless fire retreats; the wheels are asleep.

NO MORE YOURS

She is no more yours to do with: a practical
situation you already know something about.

Resolute and eager in the rain-surrounded
room, she hides her insolent delighted eyes

and moves to the half-open door.

Her modern partner leans in the passage,
courteous and mute. He has white fluent

hands for her reclining, and unambiguously
they transparently recline . . .

To the secret places not in this world I'll go,
to the various redoubts of the extinct.

DOLL'S DELIGHT

Pretty as a teacup she's
pretty as a yellow feather
floating on a maple leaf

She's cotton lionhearted
buttoned up with shells
with pins of bone her head
held stiff her eyes she's
blind but black bright
stones her eyes she's

listening unfolded ears
for two crows with a carriage
who always take her home

COMPANION FACE

I sold boxes of books; I'd read them before and after.
I dripped wine on the stones, I buried sad valentines,
and delivered my sharp rustless tools into abler hands.
But signals from the hollow house are calling me back.

Did I forget a brown bottle of a harmless love venom?
Spiders mourning the empty attic? Saucers of powders
sitting on window sills, dry grains from old moonlights?
Handcrafted argot whispering aloft and not forgotten?

Worms hang here in silk. In dreams are they dressing?
Scattered legs of a dwarf dynamo: do beetles explode?

But it's a mouse, farming waste from the littered floors,
and wrapping its meager uncolored nut-scraps of nothing
with photos of your final and aged companion face. Dust-
veiled when I struck this camp, alas — shreds only now.

A MEMORIAL

I wish I'd kept more of your face and your voice,
from the days when we thought each other comely
and fit, unafraid of felicity. For you were a witness
to my wonder when that handsome figure of discord
darkened the doorway, a lost luminous new woman
bemused by me. She was tangled, and she sought
border wars. Sometimes, remember,

I huddled with you, to own my disquiet with this
powerfully destitute and prodigal woman, who had
dared Vermont mud, who had bet everything on one
factious male stranger, and him nerved in taverns
by doubts and treasons. You asked *If it won't solve – ?*
But into her ornate nest I was gravely lifted – I was,
in my disordered way, destined to learn.

You knew when hard troubles started. All the toys
in the toy house raged. You stepped out of the traffic.
I guess your flower face has now a new pearl stead-
fastness. I don't know your family's house or its fire,
know nothing of what grace sustains you. But if ever
we enter the world together again, I will salute you
for that gift of witness, so long ago.

for M

THINK WHERE IT COULD BE

I've studied the houses and nations of death,
and their achievements – one canceled man
equals weeping on seven hills.
Haven't found the clean quiet end I've earned –
found only world-wide & wonderful calamities.

In this final house, in these latest days, I gnaw
at the future: I know how there's a pearl inside,
to be touched like a switch.
Death works its passage, anchors and settles,
begins its inquiries. I think where it could be.

Not there in the restive neglected soul, not here
in the poem's insistent unavailing tumescence,
not memorized, not forgotten.
I have a small fence for small sheep: them with
no wolf, me with no plague. Well-doctored man.

I haven't got webs in my eyes. No ebony moths
fly out of stones – as if it's not really death at all.
I know it is. I know it will be.
I take worlds apart like houses, to see can I see
any sign: I see no sign. Think where it could be.

SOME FINAL QUESTIONS

SHORT-CUTTING HOME

I crossed the field,
short-cutting home.
Just done snowing –
I wanted my boots
to make clean prints
to keep until thaw
or new snow filled
them again. Halfway
I stopped, looked
back at my trail.

I saw the world had changed.

There was a bird
in every footprint.
Into boot-packed
snow a sparrow
quietly dropped.
My path was a long
black dotted line:
dotted with birds,
small winter birds,
sparrows, titmice,
chickadees and
nuthatches. Each
stood one-legged:
one leg folded in
feathers, then stood
on the warm leg,
tucking the other
away in its breast.

No sound. Black eyes watching.

I saw assemblies,
flocks in the sky
waiting to fall. Not

one missed. Spread
braking wings and
settled my tracks.
I clapped my hands –
some birds jumped,
fell back. The day
was old, cold.
Abruptly I turned,
went on my way.

Half a mile is nine hundred paces.

Unfrightened
watchful streaked
sparrows followed,
filling my boot prints,
porch, porch steps.
Watched as I moved
to my house
in the dusk.

Birds steadfast and silent and still.

How do they know.
How do the birds know.

A PRACTICED SUBLIME

We woke at dawn and went up the river again.
Lake islands seemed floating a foot off the water.
Hemlock and spruce with high green skirts
marked the crest of spring floods.

Yesterday a locked beaver dam stopped us; we heard
beaver kits crying in the round-house. We saw a deer
to its knees in the shallows, carefully taking the lilies.
The river was black, and never a bottom.

White sun in splinters climbed the black branches.
We wordlessly moved, in a long-practiced sublime,
you in front to see everything first: kingfishers and
gray jays, muskrat, one day an eagle.

Mallards mumbled, looped in their duckweed pools.
No bears, older than ice, nor four kinds of trout, vivid
and swift, did we see that morning. We idled, paddling
to stay in one place. Then let go,

spun around; the river shouldered us downstream.
Mist lifted from marshes and lake waters. Our canoe
we tied on top of the car. Here was a lean jack rabbit
with ticks in its ears, calm as a beggar,

regarding me with all the wit of the place in its eyes.
We put the car on the road. The lake was flint, but now
it tilted in planes of yellow and green. We watched,
as long as we could, as long as it was there.

GOLDEN FIDDLEHEAD

You see she has a tail. Although this is
unusual, it's not unknown: of its kind
here is the perfect instance. It tops
the doubled handfuls of her buttocks.

Where it starts at the backbone's end
it's thick as a thumb and tapers quickly
down its twenty inches to a golden
fiddlehead, all wrapped in short soft fur.

She folds it modestly between her legs
and curls the end on her belly, or in
trousers it slips down her thigh, where
the tip just tickles the back of her knee.

AN IVORY FOR BEES

Spring dinner, deep in the garden,
by the sway and the tock of rose canes:
you and I in our splendid outfits –
lavender shirts, mauve denim overalls,
silvery lace-up Assyrian boots, our
chromium battered harmonicas stuffed
in our lavender pockets, if someone
desires a song. Roses bow in the evening,
peach streaked with amber and ginger,
or lazy white yellow-tinged petals
that gleam like an ivory for Bees.

First spoonful – and here is the Bear,
black unexpected eclipsing attendant,
trailed by a trio of gaunt blond Coyotes.
Bear chooses a chair, Coyotes sit stiff
on the bricks: they've only brought
small yelps and itchings. Whole heart,
you and I: we plaster the Bear
with a pie and wing the Coyotes with
meat-on-the-bone: feast redesigned,
but splendid withal. Scores of bowls,
scores of plates, wines bladed and tart.
Now thumps down the path one buck
Cottontail, soon dazedly sipping your
cold clover soup and triangle of toast.
A genteel and dirty large Tortoise
comes out of the west – you balance
a blue antique plate of sweet greens
on his shell; he retires (you blessing
his foreign and glass-fragile dignity) –
retires in his cuirass to the thyme bed,
there eating salad with prehistory jaws.

Squirrels who rob campsites in daylight
contentedly collar our cups full of dates.
A Porcupine needs two bamboo canes for

his walking; breaks his diet of pebbles
and twigs for a dozen sweet lemon drops.
Hilarious schoolrooms of Blackbirds and
Crows find the nut plate, and hammer-
and-anvil the nuts on the mossed russet
bricks. Wasps taller than us but aged,
slow-moving, draw their spectacles forth
to study the board: now half-empty,
half-full. All entertained, and none
disinvited, and enough for ourselves.

Bear burps and Coyotes burp thrice.
My boots are splashed with ice cream;
the bib on your bibbed overalls took
handprints from Raccoons and Otters
in your lap eating cookies. Now Bear
and Coyotes are barking for music.
Some temperaments and types stay
apart – Tigers and quartets of Hyenas,
naming a few, amiable and natural
storytellers but now and then venture
a bite, and so safer in the ball field's
outfield, beyond the yellow street light.
Now every pulse and each hunger
is rested. From lavender pouches
we slide forth the dented harmonicas,
make a note of our moods, check colors
and humors, walk out past the cloud-
nested moon, for a minute, then float
a capriccio in the spirit of Unlikeness.

White roses have tendered their yellow-
tinged petals: an ivory for Bees, but
Bees stayed away! We never knew why.
May be in their old crowded houses
some Bees were all hours at work and
balance of Bees were tired, and slept.

UNLIKELY APPLES

This late, and the logic's sad.
I held you hungry,
like others did.

Now is my house disordered,
in its hundred corners
uncorrected.

I long for the summer nights.
The copper-flavored
lemonade drips

from the cistern on the roof.

Late traffic yellows up the street.
The cat puts by its tail
until spring.

Saddest place is to be in the past,
in somebody else's
forgotten long ago.

So autumn stalls, even if its colored
songs are done, even
if the plates and cups are ice.

Flakes of sorrow in every man's clay
I've seen, no matter
if it was a careful potter.

As I do, I'll sleep through the cold,
then hurl my staff
into April water.

Here once more for summer, I guess.
Here again for its unlikely apples.

FAR FARM

I hear you tenant once more the far farm,
that remote steading where I don't know
the customs, and won't from the dirt road
solicit your attention. But I do see all other:
tree house and brass pasture bell that rings
when you rhyme. Stout palings wrap around
the circular meadow. All flowers and vines
in the world that bloom, bloom here. Red
edges, soft finish of foxes flash by. Long ago
we must once have kissed. Until I paused
here, I never slowed down to reckon the loss.

THE OLD DOCK

We'll find the dirt road, we'll find the old dock
grown wild in weeds, ruined canoes half full of
rain, rising, falling like keys on a player piano
in ripe sour waters, in perpetual green shade.
Moving past and through one
another, we'll find the old dock.

No sand path now to the cockeyed porch steps,
unleveled by subsiding brick piers the earth has
received. Brush dust off the windows. The rooms
echo, though we make no sound. Tipped tables,
torn menus, buried news on the floor:
we'll come back for the lake's blue news.

We'll come to the log lodge as it sinks in sunned
cedar and spruce, white skies calling the time,
but soft and unheeded. At sunset we'll return
with the swallows, prowl perished cabins, wing-
tip each surface. Certain we'll come
back to blue pools with the swallows.

I'm still framed; I can still vanish and reappear.
I'm clothed, I'm painted, I still drink the water,
but you – you're nothing – handful of vapor now.
I'll see you again at Blue Mountain Lake, when
I'm feathers in the storm and you –
a dozen atoms on the lake's fine skin.

SOME FINAL QUESTIONS

What is this file of babies and children crossing the river?
Is my mother their mother
Is there ever clear water
What part of his doctorate plated my father all over in brass?
Did he snap shut at night
Did she ever unbolt him
Why did he roll on his rusty wheeled platform all over town?
Was it part of his War
Did I noisily not know him
How was it that any dust storm could puncture my brother?
Was he just looser dust
Did he fade from the camera
Was he one of those pairs of which only one member exists?
Wouldn't he know me
Wasn't my fright his beacon
Where is the uncut yellow field we ran through to the river?
Was it just color on paper
Did we fall down and get up
Did I tell it at school that my father's eyebrows were briars?
Was he anciently holly
Was he a King among oaks
Why did our dogs hate us and spite us and then turn to stone?
Were we all prehistoric
Did we drink oil from the can
What stones in his first years broke my born brother in two?
Did I see – was it me
Did the years prove his wounds
For what reason the whole family wore eye-masks in museums?
Did we owe Van Gogh money
Did erect columns shame my mother
How could my brother be numb and hateful at once, two beats?
Was in his head a wrong clock
Could it have been set right
Did my father read science fiction for motives and instructions?
Did he stay a long time

Did he stay away a long time
How could he embrace the mad dog that attacked him and fled?
Did he whistle it home
Was it me

RE-SHARPENED AXE

I'm here after all with my re-sharpened axe,
thousands of words tied up, waterproofed.

Unfinished, it cracked at a seam, at a fold
in the jive – but I patched it and sanded
the fault, and now those lines are fitter than
what never was stressed, I hope and believe.

I unfurled it into the wind – some epithets
fell, some rhythms were riddled. I doctored
with waxed cord, handfuls of bronze rivets,
and so far it keeps – it keeps speaking itself.

I'm sure the ash haft of my axe, as it were,
is fitted securely to the iron eye in the head,
as it were, of the blade – burnished and oiled.
Ready for the twenty-one days of the Sagas.

MARINE

I'm not ready for the sea, but here its business is all
around me. Not ready for its sovereign uniformities:
I look for landmarks on the tides and see nothing
there, no boats or swimmers.

Unready for the million springing waves, the stones
made smooth by hammering, or the lasting movement,
back and forth, and up and down. I'm no sailor but
I know that someday, I will sail.

Melted ice now keeps the sea bleak to its harsh degree,
and sea's assaults tear houses nightly from these cliffs.
Not ready for the sea, but here potent and implacable
it's everywhere around me.

THIS VIKING

Wrap it in that old green blanket.

Find a gypsy with a fast boat.
Out of sight of land and houses,
put it on the raft with green pine
branches: pour alcohol, pour
paraffin –

making limbs and body luminous.

Cut the rope, pole away the raft.
Make a man throw burning rags.
It should all be done in daylight,
out of sight of land and houses.
It can be done within the law but

come back after dark, in any case.

THE TREE IN THE PICTURE

Once you've studied the tree in the picture,
every rock, beast and bird, every wind, water,
flower you'll know, all the deeps, all the stars.
You'll know the oceans are salted with tiny
green wheels. Leagues deep in a glowing mud
the primary membranes roam the silts,
collecting their senses and learning their food.

High tides leave pilgrims bound for the lifting
inlands. All sequences, all wins and losses are
deduced from a small colored page, unloaded
from infinite art. You'll reach them, hale and
final: man's 80-year muscles, chiseling his
journals in stone to background drums. All
doing ever is *break-neck* and *hold on* and *wait*
and *retreat:* those are the measures, no others.

But not all will be shown if hallowed lives are
not shown: animal homes in bracken and bog,
men judging a timber, high towers with choirs,
children fevered by books – even steel craves
grace now that cars are being shot to the stars.

The last unsoiled truth the tree in the picture
reveals: every fair part and rare moment
burns back to black glass.
Just from the picture, you know right away.

LEGACY

1.
Somewhere find red banners hung in the trees where
I laid down on paper a poem or a story, best I could do:

and yours now, you who may be eyed like flies and dulled
from hauling our waste out of your ways –
save for the one or two canny men and women
still attentive to the dead, to praise and ridicule the dead.

2.
A thousand words to model Centre Street in Boston,
a Friday, two thousand four: woman walking
in a yellow scarf carrying three foil-wrapped burritos
on a paper plate. Hardware store floors squeak like birds.

Or at Grand Canyon a turtle on its back, balanced on an
eggshell, or in Mattapoisett a lover's gesture
turns the sea from gray to blue. Witness I sought
other worlds: see in their thousands my failed fantasies.

3.
I drop these journals on the path to the unknown future.
Men and women, puzzling at their benches,
maybe in narrower academies, will tease from them
their customary measured praise and ridicule of the dead.

I send these gazettes to one not yet human, who may share
certain atoms lifted from the fire I'll become,
lapsed into soil, then drawn up into fruit. Numbered
and notched, those atoms will ever bide, still faintly myself.

SAY THESE WORDS

Next time you get away safe
bow your head
  whatever the danger
  however the rescue
and with your eyes closed
say these words –

Next time your father is dead
bow your head
  keep him talking
  let him own you
and with your eyes closed
say these words –

Next time it's a beautiful woman
Next time it's a bountiful man
bow your head
  let it be morning
  let there be snow
and with your eyes closed
say these words –

Next time you close with the stars
bow your head
  naming infinite alphas
  carving sapient spirals
and with your eyes closed
say these words –

Say these words
Say these words